Zelda's Bloopers

Other Books by
Carol Gardner and Shane Young

Zelda Wisdom

The Zen of Zelda

Zelda Rules on Love

Zelda's Survival Guide

Zelda's Tips from the Tub

Also by Carol Gardner

Bumper Sticker Wisdom

Zelda's Bloopers

The Good, the Bad, and the Whatever

Carol Gardner and Shane Young

**Andrews McMeel
Publishing**

Kansas City

Zelda's Bloopers

05 06 07 08 09 TWP 10 9 8 7 6 5 4 3 2 1

ISBN-13: 978-0-7407-5469-2
ISBN-10: 0-7407-5469-6

Library of Congress Control Number: 2005924759

ATTENTION: SCHOOLS AND BUSINESSES
Andrews McMeel books are available at quantity discounts with bulk purchase for educational, business, or sales promotional use. For information, please write to: Special Sales Department, Andrews McMeel Publishing, 4520 Main Street, Kansas City, Missouri 64111.

To err is human ...but it feels divine.
—Mae West

Born a Blooper

If you've ever watched one of those TV blooper shows, you know how funny slipups, gaffes, and blunders can be. I've always thought of bloopers as mistakes that were left on the cutting-room floor—but when viewed later were even better than the original shots.

I can relate. Overweight, triple chin, wrinkles, bloodshot eyes, doggy breath, an ingrown tail, short stubby legs, and an under bite orthodontists dream about. It would take most people a lifetime to look as bad as I do. But that's how I entered the world ... born a blooper. I learned, very early on, how to turn my disadvantages into advantages. If you are born a blooper, it doesn't mean you can't become a "BABE!" It's up to you to turn your disadvantages into advantages.

In this, my sixth book, I share some behind-the-scenes photographs: the bloopers ... the ones that weren't perfect at first glance, the ones we had filed as rejects. We've combined our original images with our blooper images to create a new kind of Zelda book. In Zelda's Bloopers we also share a new kind of Zelda Wisdom—a wisdom that shows how we can turn our flubs and flaws into something great.

So remember, when you make a mistake, it's okay. Take a second look. Maybe it isn't a mistake at all, but an opportunity. My wisdom says ... if you don't make mistakes, you won't make anything.

Be happy,
Zelda

In order to win . . .

you've got to be willing to lose.

Exotic vacation ahead? Remember . . .

just don't drink the water!

Sometimes you've got the balls.

Other times you just cover them and pray.

I may have to take orders . . .

but there's only so much @#*! I can take.

I'm reasonable.
You can get it to me today or . . .

YESTERDAY!

I may not be able to manage my liquor,
but . . .

I can sure lick my manager.

In life and in golf . . .

sometimes you end up in the "ruff."

No-bull intentions.

But temptation can be trou-bull.

Take time to stop and smell the flowers.

But not during the photo shoot.

Chapter Two

Some Are Born to Be Supermodels, Others Just Try to Fit into the Outfits

There are days when I feel on top of my tights.

Other days I'm just tutu pooped
to pirouette.

Worth the weight.

But what a waist!

When someone makes fun of your hat . . .

just flip 'em the bird.

I'd never vote you off my island.

Yet!

I want a man really bad.

Are you really bad?

What once was groovy . . .

is now just droopy.

Queen's Rules: Look wise, say nothing . . .

and never let them see you sneeze.

Chapter Three

It Takes Two to Tangle

Mom's first lesson . . .

Don't start by putting a foot in your mouth.

Too much of something good . . .

is simply exhausting!

Maybe if I just close my eyes . . .

he will go away.

Remember, darling, it's "Gone with" . . .

not "Break with" the Wind.

Though we don't always agree . . .

we know when to kiss and make up.

I don't know how to tell you this, but . . .

you might consider a bikini wax.

Life may be a jungle, but remember . . .

there's only one KING, and I'm it!

Love forever.

Easy? Never.

Friends savor sunny times and . . .

Stick together until...
THE END.